# RECLAIMING
# THE
# BLOOD

DR. VALERIE ARTHUR

ISBN: 978-1-66786-436-5 (Paperback)

Printed in the United States of America

# *DEDICATION*

To my mother who encouraged and supported me to pursue my dreams of becoming…and instilled in me the righteousness of Jesus and the power of an education.

To my father who gave me the ideal example of persistence who often stated, "Want it so bad that you can taste it."

To my siblings, we lift each other up, no one is left behind.

To my children and my grandchildren, there is no greater love than the love God has given me for you.

# *FOREWORD*

In her book, *Reclaiming the Blood,* Valerie Arthur has offered some essential insight. It is a must-read and a return to Biblical material that matters. Her ministry over the past twenty years has developed from her life's experience. It is now come full circle in this journey to reclaim the revelation of the blood of Jesus.

Arthur encountered the brokenness of humanity while working for almost three decades in the Department of Corrections. And now shares what is missing in the lives of sinners and the arsenal of saints. Through this book, she recognizes the eternal goodness and mercy of God.

Dr. Arthur calls into question the misrepresentation of God's power through the failure to understand the blood of Jesus. She is an important voice and a vessel who speaks the truth. This book causes the reader to reflect on God's plan by outlining scripture emphasizing the relevance of the *blood* through specific examples while associating it to this present day.

Dr. Arthur masterfully pens a book that will revolutionize how we examine blood throughout scripture. This work is transformative in reclaiming the blood's meaning and manifestation, leading the church back into its rightful place with God. Those fortunate enough to read this book will gain strength anew to *run this race,* knowing that through the power of God and the blood of Jesus, they are free from the power of sin.

The significance of the shedding of blood throughout biblical history is vital to the faith of those who profess Jesus Christ as Lord and Savior. From Genesis to Revelations, the blood symbolizes the connectivity of humanity to God. From the shedding of the blood of Abel by his brother Cain (Gen. 4:8-10) to the victorious triumph of Jesus. The blood reminds us of the ugliness of sin and the beauty of God's redemptive power.

The author provides a true testimony through her insightful account and her charge to believers to *reclaim the blood* for the present generation. This book recaps the significance of the blood and its transcending power. Her powerful work hearkens believers to reestablish their rightful place through God's covering: *the blood*. Dr. Arthur discusses how the blood allows believers to commune with God (1 Corinthians 11:28) and justifies them through faith from past sins, whereby they are made righteous (Romans 3:25).

Today, the blood of our brothers and sisters is still crying out to God. The enemy has distracted many who, like Esau, have conceded their rightful place in the kingdom. Dr. Arthur is a beacon of light who guides believers facing tumultuous times in their lives back to the Blood of Jesus.

Her steadfastness and obedience to God as a modern-day apostle are admirable. She continues to exemplify her true calling impacting the lives of those whom she encounters. It is a delight to see this woman of God continue to, *"Cry aloud, spare not, lifting her voice like a trumpet"* (Isaiah 58:1) to reclaim the blood!

Allen and Benita Patterson
Greater Harvest Church
Trenton, NJ

# *PREFACE*

In his book, *Alien Entities. A Look Behind the Door to the Spirit Realm,* Lester Sumrall, a world-renowned pioneer of deliverance ministry, describes the story of Clarita Villanueva, a young Filipina woman who was demon possessed.[1] According to him, the demon had taken over the young woman. She had cursed God the Father, God the Son, and God the Holy Spirit, and then cursed the blood of Jesus all in perfect English. Later, Pastor Sumrall would tell others that it almost seemed, by the way the demon cursed the blood of Jesus, that the demon believed the blood of Jesus was alive.[2]

Recognizing that the life of God is in the blood of Jesus, there is no wonder how the demon reacted to the blood. He knows the power of the blood of Jesus and as always, he will do anything and everything possible to blind Christians to its truth. I often tell people that the world gets it. Satan also

---

[1] The term "demon", "devil", and "Satan" are used interchangeably throughout this text.
[2] Sumrall, Lester (1995). *Alien Entities. A look behind the door to the spirit realm.* Printed in the US by Whitaker House (PA), 1995, pages 131-138

gets it so why is the church slow in understanding this truth? Could this be because the believers, those of whom I will call Christians in name only, refuse to have anything to do with what is often called, "A slaughterhouse religion"?

My purpose for writing this book is not to provide statistical data in support of the varying views embodied by those who proclaim Christianity, as this is not a book of research but one to introduce the blood of Jesus and its importance to the unbeliever, the new believer or to reclaim that which was stolen from the believer.

Therefore, I am driven to enlighten our brothers and sisters of the faith who believe that Jesus' dying on the cross was only a symbol of God's sacrifice that that belief is a myth. The truth is God's sacrifice of His only Son is real. It was an actual sacrifice through which we all benefit by the Blood of Jesus that speaks to and for us all. Thus, it is my hope that this book will serve as a resource for those who might have temporarily lost their way, may need help in finding their way, or for those who might simply find that they need a quick reassurance of the power of Jesus' blood.

# TABLE OF CONTENTS

# *Chapter One: The Blood Speaks*

*"His Spirit answers to the blood
And tells me I am born of God,
And tells me I am born of God."*[3]

As I champion the authority of the blood of Jesus and
its dominance in the life of the believer, I am struck by the fact
that there are brothers and sisters of the faith who believe that
"A loving Yahweh would not develop a system of animal
blood sacrifice as an atonement for humanity nor would He
send His own Son to shed His own blood to become the
unspeakable sacrifice once and for all, for all of humanity, past
present and future. However, they agree that some sort of
sacrifice is needed, yet it does not necessarily have to be by
blood. When I first came across this teaching, I did not believe

---

[3] The song Book of the Salvation Army #c129
https://hymnary.org/hymn/SBSA1986/c129

1

that Christians could believe such fallacies when the Word of God teaches just the opposite.

In His own words, God teaches that in Him we have redemption through His blood and the forgiveness of our trespasses, according to the riches of His grace (Ephesians 1:7). While Christ had never sinned, God treated Him as a sinner so He could make us acceptable to God. (2 Corinthians 5:21). Nonetheless, this foundational corner stone of the Christian faith is often challenged by Christians irrespective of God's grace and mercy. In fact, there are numerous articles and posts that confirm the misguided beliefs of those who profess Christianity yet oppose the power of the blood.

One such article refers to a commentary written by Roger Oakland titled *Faith Undone: The Emerging Church… A New Reformation or an End-Time Deception.* In Chapter 11 titled "Slaughterhouse Religion?", Oakland says he wrote the chapter to shine a light into darkness and to show where the emerging church is headed. "Some emerging church leaders *do* say they love the Cross, but an underlying theme is gaining momentum among them. It says Jesus going to the Cross was an example of sacrifice and servanthood that we should follow; but the idea that God would send His Son to a violent death for the sins of mankind—well, that is not who God is. A loving God would never do that! Such a violent act would make Christianity a "slaughterhouse religion."[4]

In his commentary, Mr. Oakland goes on to quote liberal theologian and pastor of the Riverside Church in New York City, Harry Emerson Fosdick (1878-1969), who authored such works as *The Modern Use of the Bible,* in which he wrote that , "Jesus going to the Cross should be seen as an example of a life of service and sacrifice and not compared with 'old animal sacrifices' and made to be 'a pious fraud' played by God upon the devil." He believes that the doctrine of the atonement, where "Jesus suffered as a substitute for us" because of our sins, is a "precivilized barbarity."[5] In another book authored by Mr. Fosdick titled *Dear Mr. Brown,* he states, "Too many theories of the atonement assume that by one single high priestly act of self-sacrifice Christ saved the world. And ends it with a pronounced[6] No!" He insists, "These

---

[4] Beka Horton, Church History and Things to Come (Pensacola, FL: Pensacola Christian College, 1997 printing), p. 156.
[5] Harry Emerson Fosdick, The Modern Use of the Bible (New York NY: The Macmillan Company, 1924), p. 230.
[6] Harry Emerson Fosdick, Dear Mr. Brown, op. cit., p. 135.

legalistic theories of the atonement are in my judgment a theological disgrace."[7] He also names Brian McLaren who currently follows the ideologies of Fosdick and Episcopal priest Alan Jones as two leading voices in the bloodless movement.

I share these references to make clear that the Bible warns us that thoughts of the kind espoused by the aforementioned authors were inevitable but reminds us that we must remain vigilant and steadfast. We must read the Word of God daily and not succumb to the tactics of the enemy that have existed for many years. In fact, Satan began to plant lies and deceit at the very tomb of Jesus, and he used religious folks to do it even back then. Therefore, this not only demonstrates that these are not new tactics of the enemy but serve to highlight the extreme efforts that Satan will undertake to stand in the path of the righteous.

As I address demon activity as it relates to the blood of Jesus, it is only appropriate that I address its highly controversial relationship with deliverance ministry. Deliverance ministry is the act of tearing down spiritual

---

[7] Ibid., p. 134-135.

strongholds in individuals' lives and releasing them from the clutches of demonic and evil influences. While not accepted by everyone, let's say for the sake of argument that I am a firm believer of deliverance ministry, as most Christians, reportedly, are. Yet, I remain surprised at how little is taught about the importance of the Blood of Jesus to deliverance ministry. No seasoned or experienced deliverance minister would cast out demons without faith in the Blood of Jesus, for it is a weapon we have received as a gift to dethrone and cast out the enemy. Similarly, it has gifted us with eternal inheritances, including the guarantee of protection from evil. Psalms 35:1-2 teaches us to pray for deliverance through the blood of Jesus by asking God to contend "…with those who contend with [us]; fight against those who fight against [us]", and "Take up shield and armor; arise and come to [our] aid."

This protection through the blood of Jesus secures in us the knowledge that the blood speaks to Yahweh. The blood cries out to God, on our behalf! Sin is covered because the penalty is paid. There is biblical evidence that all shed blood speaks to God. After the murder of Abel by his brother Cain, we read in Genesis 4:8-10, "And Cain talked with Abel his brother: and it came to pass, when they were in the field, that Cain rose up against Abel his brother, and slew him. And the Lord said unto Cain, where is Abel thy brother? And he said, I know not: Am I my brother's keeper? And He said, what hast thou done? the voice of thy brother's blood crieth unto me from the ground."[8] The life that was in Abel's blood did not cease after his death but cried out for vengeance. This may be difficult for some to understand or even to comprehend. But Yahweh is telling us that innocent-shed blood cries out to Him for vengeance.

I cannot even begin, to account for the innocent blood shed by cruel, merciless, selfish, blood thirsty, greedy people. Although the United States of American proclaims to be a country established and rooted in the principles of the Christian faith, she, too, is not guiltless in crimes involving the shedding of innocent blood. There is a cry for vengeance that rises to the ears of Yahweh. Daily the cry for vengeance gets louder and louder, the cry of the massacred Native Americans, those who fell victim to the brutality of the transatlantic slave trade, the 63 million plus abortions performed in American since 1973, the

---

[8] *The Holy Bible: King James Version*. (2009). (Electronic Edition of the 1900 Authorized Version., Ge 4:8–10). Bellingham, WA: Logos Research Systems, Inc.

children murdered due to child trafficking, victims of gang violence, lives lost to domestic violence, and mass shootings, particularly mass shootings of innocent school children. We cannot overlook those who have contended for the faith. The Bible is clear about Yahweh's vindication on behalf of the innocent.

"But as for the cowardly, the faithless, the detestable, as for murderers, the sexually immoral, sorcerers, idolaters, and all liars, their portion will be in the lake that burns with fire and sulfur, which is the second death." (Revelation 21:8 ESV); "Whoever sheds the blood of man, by man shall his blood be shed, for God made man in His own image." (Genesis 9:6 ESV). "They poured out innocent blood, the blood of their sons and daughters, whom they sacrificed to idols of Canaan, and the land was polluted with blood." (Psalm 106:38 ESV); "There are six things that the Lord hates, seven that are an abomination to Him: Haughty eyes, a lying tongue, and hands that shed innocent blood, heart that devises wicked plans, feet that make haste to run to evil, a false witness who breathes out lies, and one who sows discord among brothers." (Proverbs 6:17-19 ESV); "Lest innocent blood be shed in your land that the Lord your God is giving you for an inheritance, and so the guilt of bloodshed be upon you." (Deuteronomy 19:10 ESV).

The blood of the innocent cries out to Yahweh and He hears. In Hebrews 12:24, Paul refers to the blood of Jesus by comparing it with that of Abel's by calling it, "the blood of sprinkling, that speaks better things than that of Abel's." Whereas Abel's blood cried for vengeance, Jesus' blood cries for mercy. This is the shadow revealed from the Old Testament when the High priest went into the Holy of Holies every year and sprinkled the mercy seat the blood of bulls and goats (Hebrews 9:7). As a result, Yahweh manifested His Shekinah Glory over the mercy seat when He spoke to the high priest.

To plead the blood of Jesus is to confess to Yahweh that we are depending wholly on His mercy. When we plead the blood of Jesus, it immediately pleads for us, because it is speaking blood. It speaks of mercy from the mercy seat in heaven where Jesus is seated on the right hand of Yahweh making intercession for us, pleading on our behalf. Therefore, we plead the blood of Jesus.

It is my belief that we would begin to see the restoring of the signs, the wonders, and the miracles that we are so desperately longing to see return to the body of Christ if the church learned the value of using the blood of Jesus or remembered to honor the blood of Jesus by reclaiming it from the world and not just using it as a cliché. I can recall as a child how we would sing the blood songs diligently and with such vigor and reverence that Yahweh responded to our pleas with a manifestation of His glory by filling the building so heavily with the signs, wonders, and miracles of His presence right before our very eyes.

One such miracle that I recall is of a young man, who was born severely disabled; I'll call him Sister Barbara's grandson. He was in a wheelchair, unable to walk or talk, with dribbles of spit running down the side of his face. He had an apparatus of some sort connected to his throat to help him breathe. His mother was raised in the church but was not a practicing Christian; however, she knew where to bring him. When she arrived with him, the saints would consistently pray for his healing, as they pleaded (applied) the blood of Jesus for his complete recovery. His healing was a process but a complete healing, nonetheless. The last time I saw this young man he was still walking on his own, talking on his own, and breathing on his own. The power of the blood of Jesus, shed to bring healing to us all, was demonstrated through the life of this young man.

I also remember the healing of Sister Doris' throat disease. I was a kid, so I am assuming it was cancer. My pastor, Elder Johnson, along with the rest of the saints, placed her in a chair in front of the dais so the whole church could watch the healing take place. As they began to call upon the name of Jesus and plead His blood, Sister Doris began to cough and spit blood. At the sight of the blood, Elder Johnson tilted Sister Doris' head back to pour anointing oil into her mouth, as he continued to plead the blood of Jesus. Approximately, ten minutes later or so, she began to vomit a substance that appeared to be a mixture of black blood, mucus, flesh, and some other green matter, which was unidentifiable. The process continued until Elder Johnson had completed his mission, and while there was no obvious resolution to Sister Doris's medical condition at that moment, she later testified that she had been healed from her throat disease.

Yes, it is true! The blood of Jesus is powerful. It provides, healing, redemption, victory, protection and so much more, and those who reclaim and/or discover the secret of His blood shall witness signs, wonders, and miracles that they otherwise would not. As Charles Wesley, the song writer says, "The Spirit answers to the blood."

# *Chapter Two: The Value of the Blood*

Any attempt to evaluate the blood of Christ would be impossible. It is priceless! We learn from first Corinthians 6:20 and 7:23 that we were bought with a price, and that price is the blood of Jesus, which Peter calls precious. "You were not redeemed with corruptible things, as silver and gold... But with the precious blood of Christ" 1Peter 1:18 -19. The value of Jesus' blood is unparalleled. It can do for believers what no other can do. Because of Jesus Christ, "you who once were far away have been brought near by the blood of Christ." (Ephesians 2:13, NIV).

When the Temple of Solomon was dedicated on Mount Moriah, it is written that before they brought in the Ark of the Covenant, the actual count of the sacrificial sheep and oxen could not be number. (1 King 8:5; 2 Chronicles 5:6). In 1

Kings 8, we are told that a peace offering was made on behalf

of the nation of Israel, in which 22,000 oxen and 120,000 sheep

were sacrificed. So, "the king and all the children of Israel

dedicated the house of the Lord." Furthermore, only the best

animals were accepted for sacrifice by the Levites. Second

choice was not an option. Even in the mist of death and the

massive amount of blood that surrounded, this was a happy

day. It was a day of celebration and thanksgiving. However, it

would not compare to the day, centuries later, when Jesus was

crucified.

On the day Jesus was crucified, there was a plan to

break His legs to ensure suffocation. Accordingly, the soldiers

approached Jesus with the plan to do just that but realized He

was already dead. (John 19:32). Therefore, they did not break

His legs, but instead pierced Jesus' side with a spear, bringing

a sudden flow of blood and water (John 19:35). While the

amount of blood is inconsequential to that in Solomon's temple

in terms of volume, it is incomparable when compared in

value. He entered once for all into the holy places, not by

means of the blood of goats and calves but by means of His

own blood, thus securing an eternal redemption for us all. (Hebrews 9:12).

Accordingly, no amount of blood of animals in the Old Testament could have atoned for the sins of the world. The Bibles says when Jesus went from the city of Jerusalem, and crossed the Brook Kidron, the brook was red from the blood of thousands of Passover lambs. (John 18:1)[9] This would have been a reminder to Jesus of His coming journey to the cross. Yahweh called His Son to die, He opens a fountain that would flow forever and ever. (Zachariah 13:1) The blood that Jesus shed is a river that flows continuously that we may come to wash away our sins, sicknesses, and sorrow. Let me be clear, once we have been washed in the blood of Jesus, at our point of salvation, we are clean, but the river flows continuously so that we can become better people each time we ask Jesus to wash us in His blood. Think of it this way, you are a born-again believer, washed in the blood, however the sickness of arthritis or the disease of alcoholism has taken over your body. You are always privileged to come to the river, that flows consistently, that never dries, that never suffers from drought because of the

---

[9] Guzik, D. (2013). *John* (Jn 18:1–11). Santa Barbara, CA: David Guzik.

lack of pouring. Nor do you have to wait for someone to push you in the river. You can apply the precious blood of Jesus anytime and anywhere to cover you and to wash away your sickness and disease. After which, you will be a better person, a healed person, and a person with an overcoming testimony. As we honor the blood, sing about the blood, talk about the blood, and plead the blood of Jesus, Satan must and will pass over us.

The blood of Jesus is pleading on our behalf for mercy, forgiveness, pardon, healing, protection, and deliverance. We, as believers, must trust the blood that flows consistently and become even more familiar with its power. We must demonstrate the power of the blood. Before I became a correction officer, I had never held a gun or fired one. On my first day at the range, the range officer gave me a Smith and Wesson 5 caliber revolver. I was petrified. The weight of it alone felt powerful, but it was useless, because I lacked the knowledge on how to use it, and the weapon lacked ammunition. Likewise with the blood, if we lack knowledge in using our weapons, they are powerless. We are to use our weapons to tear down the kingdom of the enemy; therefore, we must understand and appreciate the of our possessions. Yahweh's army of believers have mighty weapons, weapons to bring down strongholds, the sword of the Spirit, which is the Word of Yahweh, (2 Corinthians 10:4) and by the blood, we overcome what power Satan thinks he has through the blood of the lamb and the word of His testimony. We need the blood and the word just like we need the gun, the knowledge, and the ammunition if it is to be effective for us.

King Solomon's daily animal sacrifice was not enough. No number of animals would be effective to do what Jesus did. There was no such thing as leftovers, everyday a new sacrifice was made. The blood shed yesterday could not cover the atonement for the new day. It had to be new blood, fresh blood. There had to be a new mercy extended. As the manna was picked up fresh every morning so the blood of the sacrifice had to be fresh every morning. However, the priceless blood of Jesus flows fresh every morning. It is not dead and coagulated. The daily shedding of blood in the Old Testament should bring home to us the tremendous value that God puts on blood. Without the shedding of blood there is no remission of sin (Hebrews 9:22).[15] Thanks be unto God for His unspeakable gift.[10] We are sanctified through the offering of the body of Jesus Christ once *for all.* [11]

The value of the blood is also taught by the great number of lambs slaughtered in the yearly observance of the pass over. The head of each family would bring a lamb for sacrifice unto Yahweh. According to Josephus, an ancient historian of Jewish culture and law, 10 to 20 persons could partake of a single Passover lamb. If one lamb was slain for an average of 15 persons per house, throughout the nations, then for two and a half million people at the time of the Exodus, over 160 thousand lambs was slain on that historical night when the bonds of Egypt gave way to the blood. We now read in 1st Corinthians 5:7 that Christ, who is our Passover, is sacrifice for us. No longer are we expected to take a lamb for 15 persons. Christ took our place and became our Passover lamb. We now accept His sacrifice and offer His blood by faith.

If every Christian who believes in the name of Jesus would plead His precious blood every day out loud, I believe the result would be catastrophic, and Satan's kingdom and

---

[10] *The Holy Bible: King James Version*. (2009). (Electronic Edition of the 1900 Authorized Version., 2 Co 9:15). Bellingham, WA: Logos Research Systems, Inc.

great deliverance will be felt in the church and in the nation. However, I need to emphasize the fact that any deliverance must be maintained. And it can only be maintained if the person meets the criteria by keeping the deliverance under the blood. I understood this perfectly when the Lord delivered me from smoking cigarettes. I heard testimony after testimony of people being delivered from cigarettes instantly, but it seemed to never happen for me. No matter how often I tried on my own it was an utter and total failure until the day that I totally submitted myself unto Yahweh. I took myself through a deliverance process by the power of the Holy Spirit and washed myself in the blood of Jesus. At this point, it has been over 20 years now and, I have not had a withdrawal or a temptation. Of course, I credit Yahweh for my deliverance. By staying under the blood by faith and obedience, I was delivered from that unhealthy habit. Correspondingly, Satan could not, I repeat Satan could not penetrate the bloodline. For when he sees the blood he must, and he does pass over. The blood of Jesus has such infinite value!

# *Chapter Three: Atonement by the Blood*

Atonement is a term that means there is an amends/reparation for a wrong or sin that has been committed. Atonement serves as a covering for our sins without which we would not have a remedy. Yahweh has provided a way for humanity to come back into harmonious relation with him (Romans. 5:20) declares, "Where sin abounds, grace did much more abound, for with grace came the blood of Jesus, which covers all sin."

Have you ever considered the last hours of the life of Jesus? Perhaps the biblical description is too repulsive for a painter such as *Diego Velazquez's Christ Crucified* to render an accurate accounting of the brutality of those last twenty-four hours. Often there is a perception of *an idealized* depiction of a man wrapped in loincloth, having very little evidence of the torture and violence endured. Crucifixion is a method of capital punishment in which the victim is tied or nailed to a large wooden cross and left to hang until eventual death. It was used as a punishment by the Romans, among others. Perhaps it is easier to accept a less dramatic history of what Jesus sustained.

Mel Gibson's *The Passion of the Christ* is perhaps one of a few accounts that closely captures the suffering of Jesus. Perhaps it is beyond our understanding to capture the magnitude of the atrocities and cruelty administered by the hands of Roman soldiers' crucifixion methods. At the time of Jesus's crucifixion, the process had been refined to execute as much pain and torture as possible. According to scripture, Jesus carried the cross to Mount Calvary. However, the prisoners carried the patibulum (the crossbar of a cross used for crucifixion) across their shoulders with their arms tied in place. When the place of execution was reached, nails were placed in the prisoners' wrists to inflict as much pain as possible. Their feet were tied to a pole so that prisoners could not lift themselves up to keep from suffocating. The sole purpose was to prolong the pain. If the soldiers so wished, one could live for a week in this condition.

Imagine suspended arms bound in place extended along the patibulum, feet raised just enough, lifting yourself as to not suffocate on the cross. Your life literately hanging in the balance at the hands of the executioner. Prisoners were without food and water as fluids escaped the body. There was no one to help. Who would dare to help? Who will hear the cries of agony? The crosses were lined as streetlights as a warning to pedestrians as they entered the cities. This was the harsh reality of Jesus' death as He hung suffering in excruciating pain, bearing the weight of humanity's sin.

In essence, Jesus satisfied the penalty for crimes he did not commit. His death represented the blood sacrifice offered for the disobedience of humanity. Jesus, like Adam, covered nakedness through the sacrifice and shedding of blood. His blood has become a covering for us. In the garden, Adam tried to cover his nakedness from God with a fig leaf, but a fig leaf and a loincloth will not do, they cannot hide our sins. Only the precious blood of Jesus can appease the judgment of Yahweh.

The Bible tells us that the Roman soldiers thrusted a crown of a dozen or more thorns almost two inches long on Jesus' head. Blood tricked down His scalp, running downward to an already matted beard. Spikes were driven into the palms of His hands as blood streamed down His arms and sides. His bones were broken (Psalm 22) and face was so badly beaten He was unrecognizable. Blood flowed from everywhere. Jesus' body, the patibulum, and the stipe were covered in His blood. The life source of Jesus slowly seeped out. from the thirty-nine lacerations. As if this was not enough, the Bible records soldiers speared Jesus in His side, causing blood to spill even more. The very earth was soaked in His blood.

Yahweh's response to Abel's blood cried out to him centuries before (Gen 4). I have heard non-believers and those of other faiths remark why would Jesus allow himself to be taken by His enemies to be hung on a cross? Why would He suffer? His answer is my response. He did it for me, He did it for you, and for the sins of the world. To cover our sins so we can be restored to Yahweh and brought back into relationship with God.

The effectiveness of the covering by the Blood of Jesus was revealed to me one night after finishing sixteen hours at Edna Mahon Correctional Facility for Women (formally Clinton Correctional Facility for Women). I was not looking forward to the one-hour drive ahead of me. It was already late, I was tired, and navigating the unlit mountainous roads would take all the energy I had remaining. To traverse in the rain would have been dangerous. I desperately wanted to head off part of Route 31 that goes through the Cushetunk Mountain and closer to the town of Flemington before the rain started. I had to hurry. The clouds were fast approaching.

I got in my car, drove out of the parking lot, and turned right onto Pittstown Road. I headed onto Highway 78 East for two miles and then turned right on to Route 31 South. About 15 minutes into my drive as I neared South Annadale, I noticed the moon disappeared, covered by dark clouds. Without warning, the clouds opened as if someone had taken buckets of water and poured them on the earth. An inconceivable thunderstorm. It was extremely dark and raining heavily. I could not see five feet in front of me. I was scared but did not have the good sense to pull over to the side of the road to wait out the storm. I just kept driving.

This stretch of highway on the mountain is only two lanes north and south. There was no room for error. As I was coming around the bend, so was an eighteen-wheeler. Although I was moving slowly, I had not noticed I had drifted over into oncoming traffic. I knew I was a goner, so I wanted to make things right with Jesus. In that moment, my only prayer was to plea the blood of Jesus and call on His name. The next thing I recalled was my little red Ford Escort hydroplaned and spun back to my side of the road. The car landed between the only opening of the guardrail at the base of the mountain. I was so thankful to Yahweh. After checking for injuries, I started my car and continued down the mountain. I knew God heard my plea and saved my life. The blood of Jesus covered me that night and many times following this incident.

If we truly understood the meaning of the word *atonement*, we discover tremendous truths. Yahweh's promise to us that He has cast our sins in the sea of forgetfulness, we are seen by Him through the lens of the righteous blood of Jesus. By faith, the blood of Jesus has covered us. Because when Yahweh sees blood, He does not see sin, He sees His Son.

Leviticus 17:11, tells us the blood is in the only offering that can make an atonement or covering for our souls. Levitical law informs that atonement was made by the shedding of blood of a sacrificial animal taking the place of the unbeliever to die in his place. A blood covering was provided for the sinner, the unbeliever, and the stranger (Leviticus 17:12).

Since the fall of Adam, the beginning of a sinful humanity, the requirement of a blood atonement was established. Blood was shed to provide protection for Adam and Eve's nakedness. Adam and Eve sought to cover themselves to maintain relationship with Yahweh. They were the creation not the creator. Only the Creator can establish and implement the operating procedures that governs the relationship between Him and His creation. The creation could not substitute fig leaves to cover nakedness. No other garments would sufficiently cover Adam and Eve, except those which involved the shedding of blood. From the beginning, a system of blood sacrifice was established. Animals were sacrificed and only after blood was shed, was atonement made. To offer anything less than salvation through the sacrifice of Jesus' blood is to offer fig leaf religion. There isn't anything we can do on our own to remedy our sin. Our efforts to become righteous will fail. As Adam and Eve experienced, when we stand before the Creator, fig leaves will not cover us. Similarly, we attempt to hide our sin with fig leaves of religious or traditional practices and rituals that cannot take the place of Yahweh's divine plan to shield us from judgment by the sacrifice of Jesus' blood.

It is imperative that we understand the importance of observing the Lord's Supper, or what is known as Communion. That we partake in both the bread which represents the physical body of Christ and the wine, which represents the blood of Christ. (Mark 14:22-25). So then in the Lord's Supper, we are to receive both the bread and wine, which speaks of Jesus, the crucified Word of God, and the blood He willingly shed. We take the bread first, and then the wine. In I John 5:8 we are told, "… there are three that bear witness in the earth, the spirit, and the water and the blood: and these three agree in one." In the Bible, water is often a symbol of the Word of God. It continuously washes us (Ephesians 5:26). The Word without the blood is useless, for the life of Jesus, the Word of God, is in the blood.

The Holy Spirit also agrees with the water and the blood. For this reason, when we honor the blood, the Holy Spirit immediately manifests Himself on our behalf. The Holy Spirit agrees with the Word of God, and with the blood of Jesus (1 John 5:7). The Father, Son, and Holy Spirit are one.

In the Old Testament on the Day of Atonement, the blood was sprinkled on the Book. Why? Because the book is lifeless to the reader unless the blood is first applied. I wholeheartedly believe that those who have not been washed in the blood may struggle to understand or comprehend the Bible. They may question its authenticity, authority, or its relevancy for the modern world. Without an understanding, our spiritual vision is dim. Both the Book and the people were sprinkled with the blood. This too was fulfilled on Calvary's cross. Jesus, who is the living Word of God, was sprinkled with His own blood.

There is power in the name of Jesus only because He shed His own blood and offered it to Yahweh the Father, who gave His power and His authority to His Son (Matthew 28:18).

That same power and authority is available to all believers (Luke 10:19); however, it only becomes activated as we honor His blood. Furthermore, when our substitute Jesus, died on the cross, He died for us. He took our place. His death was the fulfillment of God's requirement for forgiveness of sin. The Old Testament gives an abundance of evidence that sin could only be forgiven by Yahweh through the principle of sacrifice. However, The New Testament also testifies and bare witness that, "…without the shedding of blood there is no remission." (Hebrews 9:22).

Jesus was crucified at the time of Passover. Passover is the feast the Israelites had to remember the time when Yahweh said, "When I see the blood, I will pass over you." (Exodus 12: 23). Israelites celebrated the first exodus leaving the slavery bondage of Egypt while Jesus made atonement for the second exodus which is freedom from the bondage of sin and death. To all who will believe in this sacrifice and efficiency of Jesus' precious blood, there is an exodus from the penalty of sin and eternal death.

When we consider the great burden of sin and guilt bestowed on Jesus at the cross, it is no wonder His soul cried out in agony, "My God, my God, why hast thou forsaken me?" (Psalms 22:1; Matthew 27:46). So why did the Father forsake the Son? It is written that Yahweh cannot look upon sin. (Habakkuk 1:13). When Jesus was baring the sins of the world on the cross, the Father could not look at His Son. Jesus became sin for us. Jesus bore the guilt of our sin, took the punishment we deserved. The Father could not look at Jesus until the blood of the Son had been pour out and offered up as a sacrifice. His own blood. It was only after Jesus poured His blood upon the altar that the Father could behold His Son. "For the law having a shadow of good things to come, and not the very image of the things, can never with those sacrifice which they offered year by year continually make the comers thereunto perfect. For it is not possible that the blood of bulls and of goats should take away the sins" (Heb 10:1). Jesus had to apply His blood to the heavenly mercy seat to redeem humanity.

Let me explain it this way. My duties as a corrections officer afforded me many opportunities to experience the legal procedures especially those of the sentencing process. Imagine, if you will, that you were in the court room when Narik

Wilson, a/k/a "Spaz," 32, and Emil Rutledge, a/k/a "Diddy",

the leaders of Newark NJ Blood street gang set, Sex Money

Murder, appeared before US NJ District Judge Susan D.

Wigenton for sentencing; their crimes consisted of attempted

murder, conspiracy to commit murder, and conspiracy to

distribute heroin. Wilson, the leader, or "O.G." of Sex Money

Murder, admitted that he directed the murder and attempted

murder of eight rival gang members in and around Newark.

Rutledge, a "captain," or "shot-caller," of Sex Money Murder,

admitted that he and others carried out several shootings

ordered by Wilson, causing serious injuries to others and the

death of a victim. It had already been decided through a plea

agreement that they each would serve 360 months, which is a

total of 30 years behind bars.[11]  It was understood that the time

would more than likely to be served in the New Jersey State

Prison. As the judge's gavel hits the plate, she says "As is

ordered by the court."

At that very moment, as the guilty verdict is being

handed down, a complete stranger interrupts and says, "Your

Honor, they are guilty, have been convicted of all the charges

---

[11] https://www.justice.gov/usao-nj/pr/leaders-violent-bloods-street-gang-sentenced-30-years-prison-racketeering-conspiracy

of attempted murder, conspiracy to commit murder, and conspiracy to distribute heroin, and the penalty of 30 years is well deserved, but set them free. I am offering my life in exchange for theirs, to serve the penalty of 30 years, in their place. Give me their well-deserved punishment. Put the handcuffs and leg irons on me, process me, and escort me to New Jersey State Prison in their place. They are free to go. Place me in their cell. When the officers walk by, they will see me, not them." Can you image the look on everyone's faces and feel the level of intensity in the room? The shock of disbelief of Wilson and Rutledge when the cuffs come off? Before them is a person who is willing to serve a 30-year prison sentence on their behalf. A person who has not committed a crime or deserves to be in prison and by all accounts, is innocent. One who asserts, "I am willing to exchange my life and my freedom for theirs." In essence, the totality of their crimes has now been cast on to him. This situation aligns perfectly with the acts of Jesus as he is nailed to the cross not his own sins but our sins. Our sins were atoned under the precious blood of Jesus. His life for our life. The demand of the Father was met. When the Father sees the believer, He sees our righteousness through pure blood of His

Son. Jesus offered His Life in His blood for all humanity. The

Father accepted His sacrifice, and our redemption was made

complete.

# Chapter Four: The Passover and the Blood

*The Lamb's Blood*
*By Donald Lawrence*

*Forensic science teaches us*
*Life has a voice*
*One drop can identify*
*Who's committed a crime*

*Don't tell him*

*To those that can hear*
*Have no reason to fear*
*No weight on their shoulder*
*Because of the blood I'll pass over*
*Cain killed Abel*
*There was blood of the ground*
*It was blood brought up from the ground*
*Angels*

*Years later*
*Another Lamb they slay*
*But His blood cried out, forgiveness, peace*
*Protection, prosperity, mercy, healing*
*It spoke a different word than Abel's*
*Abel spoke vengeance, violence, pain, hurt*
*But Jesus' love speaks a better word than Abel's[12]*

---

[12] <u>Donald Lawrence And The Tri-City Singers</u>

The book of Genesis teaches us that animals were sacrificed unto Yahweh long before the covenant with Israel was codified into law. Yahweh shed the blood of an animal to cover the sins of Adam and Eve. Adam and Eve taught this ritual to their two sons Cain and Abel. In Genesis 8:20, Noah builds an altar after the flood on which he offered a sacrifice of clean animals and birds. Why the sacrifice of blood instead of prayer, blood offers covering and atonement for our sins. Noah offered sacrifice allowed him to enter Yahweh's presence. In Yahweh's presence, Noah could commune, pray, and worship. God only establishes relationship with us through the blood of His Son Jesus Christ. He sees and hears us through the sinless blood of Jesus. There is no other way.

Abraham, the chosen friend of Yahweh, was called from his father's house, in the city of Ur, to an unknown destination by an unknown God. Abraham was father of the Israelites who offered his only son, Isaac, the promised child born to a mother and father of their later years. It is because of Abraham the nation of Israel exits today. Israelites born in Egypt knew the story of Abraham. They were aware their very existence as a nation was a result of God's mercy in supplying a ram for sacrifice instead of the life of Isaac. They knew the importance of the blood. Although there was not codified law, the word for four hundred years was passed down from generation to generation that Yahweh requires blood. Nine terrible plagues befell upon Egypt, but still Pharaoh refused to let them go. It was by the blood that Yahweh delivered the Israelites.

God said to Moses and Aaron, "Speak ye unto all the congregation of Israel, saying in the tenth day of this month they shall take to them every man a lamb... A lamb for a house" (Exodus 12:3). It was a lamb without blemish and most valuable one in the flock to offer. Each house had a lamb. The promise is available for us today. Yahweh promises to save the entire house.

God instructed them to "...take of the blood, and strike it on the two side posts and on the upper door post of the houses wherein they shall eat it... For I will pass through the land of Egypt this night, I will smite all the first born in the land of Egypt, both man and beast... And the blood shall be to you for a token upon the house where we are; and when I see the blood, I will pass over you, and the plague shall not be upon you to destroy you…" (Exodus 12:7, 12,13.) "And ye shall take a bunch of hyssops and dip it in the blood that is on the basin and strike the lintel and the two-side post with the blood that is in the bason: and none of you should go out at the door of his house until the morning. For the Lord will pass through to smite the Egyptians; and when He sees the blood upon the lintel, and on the two-side post, the Lord will pass over the door, and will not suffer the destroyer to come in onto your houses to smite you." (Exodus 12:22-23).

If Israelites decided to venture out even to have a look in the middle of the night, even for one second, they would have perished. They would not have been under the blood but in disobedience. If they attempted to offer their own covering and not sprinkle the blood, they would have perished. If they offered anything less than the blood of the lamb without blemish, they would have perished. Anything less than what was instructed would not be acceptable. No offering or substitute man provided on its own would not have been good enough. The Israelites would have perished with the Egyptians.

Yahweh did not permit the destroyer to bring death into their homes. Who is this destroyer made impotent by the blood? Satan is the destroyer. In Revelation 9:11 we are introduced to the king of the bottomless pit. Abaddon is his name in Hebrew, and Apollyon is his Greek name, both of which means destroyer. So, the great destroyer is Satan, the king of the bottomless pit.

It is important to understand that Satan is the destroyer, comes to steal, kill, and destroy. There is no good in him. He is the author of death and misery. The Bible assures us that Yahweh is King of Kings. He alone reigns supreme, and Satan cannot bring destruction and trouble to anyone unless it is permitted by Yahweh. Even if Yahweh grants such permission to Satan to bring calamity into your life, Yahweh will work that into your blessing. Take Job for instance, with Yahweh's permission, Satan took the lives of his seven sons and three daughters, seven thousand sheep, three thousand camels, five hundred oxen, and asses, and burned down his house. Yahweh allowed boils to afflict his body, his wife instructed him to curse God and die. His extended family, neighbors, and all those who previously ate at his table walked away. Job's three closest friends condemned him. In the end, Yahweh worked it all in Job's favor and He repaid him double. "And the Lord turned to the captivity of Job, when he prayed for his friends: also, the Lord gave Job twice as much as he had before." (Job 42:10-11). Therefore, Satan does not have the last say, Yahweh does. Satan cannot do anything unless Yahweh allows.

Although Satan is the ruler of this world (John 12: 31; Ephesians 2:2), it is only the mercy of God that keeps us from the incredible power of the wicked destroying angel, Satan. It is only by our faith in Jesus and His precious blood, that we can overcome, the devil, and his demonic spirits. We are no longer subject to spirit of this world. We were once like them in times past desiring the lust of the flesh, fulfilling the desires of the flesh and the mind...but God, who is rich in mercy, for His great love wherewith he loved us, even when we were dead in sins, hath quickened us together with Christ, (we are saved by His grace) Ephesians 2:4. Let us not forget this Jesus now sits on the right hand of the Father with all power and that power he extends to us. Thus, Satan has no power over us, bless our God.

Yahweh sent the destroyer to finalize the tenth plague upon Egypt. The plague of the firstborn. The Israelites were not the only ones who cherished their first born, in fact the custom of birthing rights was not unique to Israel. The Egyptians also revered the firstborn son. The Pharoah's first-born son was a prized possession, he was heir to the throne. Along with other birthright privileges and responsibilities, caring for the elder Pharaoh in the afterlife would be the sole responsibility of the first-born son. Therefore, the death of the first born would mean the current Pharaoh would be without support in the afterlife. The cattle were also important and considered a god. Twenty-five characteristics of a perfect bull was identified to earn the status of god, being the firstborn bull was its chief characteristic.

The Bible tells us that when the destroyer saw the bloodline, the blood sprinkled on the lintels and door post of the homes of the Israelites, they were passed over. If the bloodline was not found the firstborn in every family would have perished. When the destroyer saw the blood, everything in that house including the firstborn of the cattle were saved.

It all comes full circle to atonement. When the Israelites used the hyssop to apply the blood on the lintels and door posts, Yahweh's restraining order was activated. The destroyer was not to enter. The totality of hell cannot touch those who are covered under the blood. Now that is powerful. The Israelites were completely covered. Satan was limited because of an active restraining order. If he had his way, he would have used the opportunity to destroy the Israelites.

If you have met Yahweh's criteria, the restraining order is active for you today. To accept the salvation of His Son, Jesus Christ, and walk in obedience activates the restraining order. The Israelites had to do more than believe that the blood would work. They had to obey the instructions given in order to be saved. I also believe the blood of Jesus will be the "Seal" of the Holy Spirit that is spoken of in Revelation 7:3. As believers, we are marked with an invisible seal, yet it carries great authority. A seal signifies guaranteed safety, it is a mark of ownership and certifies that something is real or authentic. We are free and bought with a price (1 Corinthians 7:22). The seal of the blood of Jesus grants us access to certain privileges not afforded to non-believers.

As believers, we have an understanding that the world will come under judgment. Just as the Israelites in ancient Egypt were set aside and sealed by the blood, in the coming judgment, the bloodline restraining order will be activated again.

"And after these things I saw four angels standing on the four corners of the earth, holding the four winds of the earth, that the wind should not blow on the earth, nor on the sea, nor on any tree. And I saw another angel ascending from the east, having the seal of the living God: and he cried with a loud voice to the four angels, to whom it was given to hurt the earth and the sea, Saying, hurt not the earth, neither the sea, nor the trees, till we have sealed the servants of our God in their foreheads." (Revelation 7:1-3)

I am convinced that Satan cannot stand before the blood of Jesus when it is honored, nor can he cross the bloodline if we are in obedience with Yahweh. It is when we choose to move away from the protection of the blood that we subject ourselves to the ill intent of Satan and judgment of God. The promise of protection, healing, cleansing, covering, salvation are ours. Yahweh will not remove it from us; however, we can choose to walk away from being protected. Satan seeks to draw us out from the blessings and promises of God.

I refer you back to the story of Balaam. In the book of Numbers, we are introduced to Balaam, the son of Beor a prophet, who was commissioned by Balak son of Zippor, king of Moab to curse the children of Israel. Balak feared Israel and wanted to stop the blessing upon their lives. Balaam attempted three times to curse the Israelites but every time he opened his mouth to curse them, a blessing from Yahweh would come forth. This angered Balak.

Balaam understood the only way to curse a blessed people was to persuade them to walk away from protection on their own. "The men of Israel were camped in Shittim and began to indulge in sexual immorality with the Moabite women who invited them to perform sacrifices to their gods. The people ate the sacrificial meal and bowed down before these gods. The Israelites attached themselves to Baal of Peor and the Lord's anger burned against them." Numbers 25:1-3 In this instance, not only did the women seduce the men of Israel, but they were also encouraged by the prophet Balaam. The people of God were led astray. Yahweh loves us so much that He is willing to forgive us just as He did the children of Israel. He is willing to receive us back if we turn from our wicked ways and call upon His name.

## Chapter Five: Reclaiming the Blood

Satan's agenda is to steal, kill, and destroy. (John 10:10). The Bible describes Satan as the enemy of humanity who prowls like a roaring lion to wreak havoc on our lives by corrupting everything that is holy, righteous, and ordained by God. He convicts and condemns and is a master deceiver. He has done a most brilliant and clever campaign of convincing the lost he does not exist. His nonexistence suggests there are no consequences for sin. If there are no consequences, the world is free to do as it will without restraint. What is sin? Sin is being out of the will of Yahweh's plan for your life.

Satan's plan has not changed; it is the same deceptive one presented in the Garden of Eden to Adam and Eve. Now the serpent, the instrument or tool of a higher agent, was more subtle than any beast of the field God made. Satan's first seed of deception was to have humanity to put the Word of Yahweh into question. When the serpent noticed Eve doubt Yahweh's word, he became bolder in his assertions. Not only did Satan seize the opportunity to affirm Eve's seed of uncertainty, but he also implied she would be without impunity.

The serpent planted seeds of doubt into the mind and heart of humanity. We must remember Satan once was a servant and stood in the very presence of the Most High God, having privilege and access to the very throne of Yahweh. He himself had a relationship with Yahweh. Satan once privy in his servitude to Yahweh, stood in the throne room at will, until he desired the throne. Satan having full knowledge of Yahweh's sovereignty coveted this for himself. Yahweh is creator and the creation can never be the creator. Because Yahweh is eternal. He will always sit on the throne and will forever rule. Only Jesus, the first and only begotten Son of the Father, qualifies to inherits the throne. Satan's only recourse is to attempt to usurp the authority of Yahweh. So arrogant, so sure of his own abilities, Satan pursued one third of the angels to wage war in heaven to remove Yahweh from the throne (Ezekiel 28:1-10).

The Bible tells us because of sin, Satan will suffer eternal damnation and will be casted in the lake of fire into a bottomless pit. Satan desired to be Yahweh; he desired to be worshiped and to sit in the seat of the Highest. This was not the will of Yahweh. Because of Satan's sin, there is no plan of redemption available to him. His fate is sealed.

Another name for Satan in the Greek is Diabolos which means "slanderer". His aim is to destroy, by slandering God's character, a method he continues to use until this day. Satan defames the character of Yahweh and the character of those who represent him. If Satan could seduce Eve into disbelieving God's character, he could sever their relationship. After planting the seed to doubt God's word, he proceeded to slander Yahweh's character.

Tyron Edwards an American theologian of the 1800's, best known for compiling the "New Dictionary of Thoughts", a book of quotations wrote, "The slander and the assassin differ only in the weapon they use; with one it is the dagger, with the other it is the tongue. The former is worse than the later, for the last only kiss the body, while the other murders the reputation." Can you imagine the serpent whispering in Eve's ear? "And the serpent said unto the woman, Ye shall not surely die: For God doth know that in the day ye eat thereof, then your eyes shall be opened, and ye shall be as gods, knowing good and evil." (Genesis 3:4-6).

The seeds have been planted and now Eve is left to make a decision, she is faced with two opposing thoughts, "And when the woman saw that the tree was good for food, and that it was pleasant to the eyes, and a tree to be desired to make one wise, she took of the fruit thereof, and did eat, and gave also unto her husband with her; and he did eat. And the eyes of them both were opened, and they knew that they were naked; and they sewed fig leaves together and made themselves aprons." (Genesis 3:6-7). Jamieson and Brown, in their contribution to the Commentary Critical and Explanatory on the Whole Bible, wrote, "His words meant more than met the ear. In one sense her eyes were opened; for she acquired a direful experience of "good and evil to steal that which belongs to Yahweh, to kill those which belong, and to destroy the relationship between humanity and Yahweh. There are men and women today that have fallen into the same lure as Eve. They know the truth but because they have questioned Yahweh's word, have questioned the power of Jesus' shed blood for the redemption of sin. They resist His plans for their lives they desire to be mini gods to themselves.

Another lie Satan perpetuates is to deceive those who acknowledge his existence into believing he is equal in power to Yahweh. He is a master illusionist deceiving humanity by weaving his agenda into to fallen systems. His self-representation of being omnipresent, omnipotent, and omniscient are fraudulent. His aim is to impersonate the one true Yahweh. He is a created being. The creation can never be equal that of the creator. He is a cursed reflection of his former self.

Contrary to popular belief, he is a fallen creation of Yahweh. Why was sin found in Lucifer's heart? Why did not Yahweh put him in the lake of fire right away? It remains a mystery. I do not have a solid biblical answer. The creator never releases all into the creation, there are some mysteries withheld. According to Ezekiel 28, Lucifer was created special. Many theologians and biblical scholars agree that Ezekiel 28 prophetical comprehensive account of the fall of Lucifer. He is depicted as the king of Tyre in verse 12. Perfect in the day of his creation, full of wisdom and perfect in beauty covered in every precious stone. "Son of man, take up a lament concerning the king of Tyre and say to him: This is what the Sovereign Lord says: " You were the seal of perfection, full of wisdom and perfect in beauty. You were in Eden, the garden of God; every precious stone adorned you: carnelian, chrysolite and emerald, topaz, onyx and jasper, lapis lazuli, turquoise and beryl. Your settings and mountings were made of gold; on the day you were created they were prepared. You were anointed as a guardian cherub, for so I ordained you. You were on the holy mount of God; you walked among the fiery stones. You were blameless in your ways from the day you were created till wickedness was found in you." (Ezekiel 28:11-15).

Satan is a master deceiver. His means of deception are powerful as he uses channels to promote fear and conflict. His life gripping tentacles reach far into the entertainment and business industries as he preys on the need to entice his victims with fame, money, and power. His demonic strategy has invaded our education and government systems. The propensity for sin becomes rooted in our bloodlines and even our religious institutions are subject to his indoctrinations. He is skillful at posing himself as omnipresent. Satan cannot be all places at the same time. Lucifer lost his first state as the anointed cherub, the light barrier, the morning star, and became the adversary of Yahweh.

It is through blood sacrifices that he attempts to achieve deception of being equal to Yahweh, having the ability to reward and cleanse those who serve him. For them the blood represents humanity's pain and death. He teaches his followers to use the blood of humans and animals to honor him and to reach higher positions in his kingdom with the promise of power and wealth. The best blood to offer him is the blood of innocent humans, the life force of Yahweh is in the blood. I recommend Dr. Rebecca Brown book *"He came to set the captives free"* for more detailed explanation.

Yet another lie and probably the most dangerous is that spiritual warfare is a metaphor for the believer's life. Believers have a lot of metaphors such as, "I'm living this life to live again.", "I'm running a race.", or "To be like Jesus." However spiritual warfare is more than a metaphor, it is a reality and has been a battle since the beginning of time as we know it. War rages between angels and demons, and kingdom of Satan and Kingdom of Yahweh. There is a battle today over the souls of humanity. If we believe it is just a metaphor, we will not be ready to engage the enemy on the battlefield.

Battles are launched all around us. It is us who must believe it is happening. Why else would Paul mention the weapons that are afforded to the believer in (Ephesians 6) for the believer to learn how to equip themselves? If Satan can convince the believer there is no such thing as spiritual battle, then we will not know spiritual weapons are available to us. We know there is power in the name of Jesus. We are acquainted with the weapons in Ephesians 6, but what about the most powerful weapon other than the Word of Yahweh? What about the blood of Jesus, the crucified one? What about the significance of the blood of Jesus Christ and symbolism of the color it represents?

Colors are also used as symbols to convey a message or social status. The Bible which is full of metaphors uses colors in ways, to communicate Yahweh's special ideas and principles to His people. For example, brown, which is mentioned in the Bible four times, all of which are in the thirtieth chapter of Genesis, are associated with earth or prosperity. White is mentioned in the New and Old Testament to represent holiness, righteousness, and purity. In a familiar scripture such as Revelation 1:14-15, Jesus is depicted as having white hair, eyes like a flaming fire (red) and feet the color of brass. "His head and His hairs were white like wool, as white as snow; and His eyes were as a flame of fire; And His feet like unto fine brass, as if they burned in a furnace;" [13] Blue represents the heavenly realm, the presence of Yahweh, and the precious Holy Spirit. Green represents life. A color rarely found in biblical days was purple, it was usually associated with royalty and wealth. Then there is Red. In the Bible, red is also called scarlet and crimson. It perhaps has the most complex meaning of all.

Red is a primary color and cannot be formulated by mixing other colors. "Oudem" means "red clay." It is also the Hebrew root word for Adam, Esau, and Edom. Red is the color of blood, which is associated with sin (Isa. 1:18), violence, war, and aggression. (Revelation 6:1-8; Nahum 2:3) It is also

---

[13] *The Holy Bible: King James Version.* (2009). (Electronic Edition of the 1900 Authorized Version., Re 1:14–15). Bellingham, WA: Logos Research Systems, Inc.

the color that symbolizes Christ's and Yahweh's work of atonement, Pentecost, redemption, and salvation plan (Exodus 12:7; 1 Peter 1:18-19; Hebrews 9:22, Leviticus17:11; 1 John 1:7; Revelation 4:2-3: Rev. 19:13-15). Red represents covenant (Matthew 26:28; Exodus 24:8; Hebrews 9:8), wealth (2 Samuel 1:24; Proverbs 31:21) and love. So, if the color red represents the work of Jesus, atonement, Pentecost, redemption and salvation, it identifies with wealth, covenant and love.

Why then did Christian denominations prohibit adorning oneself in red attire. It appears to me a choice was made to emphasize, the negativity of war, violence, and anger associated with red than with the work of the cross. More was stressed to point out the fleshly desire than attribute to the atonement of God. Colors are often used by gangs to identify themselves and their adversaries. Gang members often have identifying characteristics which are unique to their specific group. Wearing colors has long been a way for them to show solidarity. Recent data reports gangs are moving away from displaying colors because it had led to being quickly identified by law enforcement. One group, for instance, is known to wear red. This has caused some of our youth, in certain geographic locations, to abstain from wearing particular colors to avoid potential conflicts or deadly situations. Of course, not everyone who wears a distinct color is a member of a gang. Red frequently represents the blood sacrifice in the Bible. However, in gang culture, red represents the Bloods, the name of a gang affiliation.

"So why can't we wear red again?", was a question often asked by one of my younger sisters as a child, whose favorite color was red. It was perceived to be the color a Jezebel would adorn. Do you want to be a Jezebel? Jezebel! I doubt at the age of fourteen she knew Jezebel was a person in the Bible. Was this the best way to respond to a 14-year-old girl who was in the phase of self-discovery? The color red made her feel pretty and powerful. She liked it. To say to her that red is worldly, and evil is wrong and may have caused some psychological and emotional harm. Was this the only explanation? My young sister decided to be defiant and wore her red belt to church. After service, the pastor and our grandmother called her to his office to lecture her for wearing red. Following this incident, my sister was no longer interested in trusting Yahweh's people, or their church.

According to mental health studies, colors evoke our mood and emotions. They, in some unique way, illustrate our emotions and our reaction. It is also believed that our emotions are closely related to our ability to perceive our feelings and moods. Taking care of our emotional well-being is just as important as our physical well-being.

Another incident occurred during Holy Convocation when a young woman, in her early twenties, wore a red dress. She wore no stockings and donned open-toed shoes. These were all prohibited. As she rode the elevator, an elderly elder of the church entered. Apparently, he looked at her and called her a Jezebel and a harlot. She asked him why he called her a Jezebel when he didn't even know her. According to my source, she was a senior in college and youth worker in her church, yet because of her attire was judged and condemned to a burning hell to adorn herself in red. Heaven help her if she wore make up or red lipstick. This was considered too worldly, sinful, loose, and placed one in jeopardy of being excommunicated. The doors of heaven were closed. This young lady also left the church, or at least our organization.

According to mental health studies, colors evoke our mood and emotions. They, in some unique way, illustrate our emotions and our reaction. It is also believed that our emotions are closely related to our ability to perceive our feelings and moods. Taking care of our emotional well-being is just as important as our physical well-being.

Without biblical evidence, or plain old sound logic, we were indoctrinated with the spirit of fear. To wear red, was like breaking one of the ten commandments. Disobeying any commandment was to incur the wrath of Yahweh by the way of the pastor or congregation. Usually, the shaming and emotional punishment were so severe, most young people left our church.

What my young mind could not comprehend was that many of Pentecostal and Holiness churches I attended was decorated entirely in red. For instance, the carpet, seating on the pews, prayer pillows that laid at the front of the alter were all red in color. The pulpit chairs, including the pastor's seat, were all upholstered in red. If red was such an unholy color, taught to represent worldliness, sin, and prostitution, why was it also the dominate color in the sanctuary? We could not wear it yet could sit, pray, and walk on it. Jesus' precious blood is red. Jesus, make all of this make sense to me!

Years later I was invited by one of my friends in the ministry to speak at a "Women in Red" platform service. To my surprise, I did not own one article of red clothing. Although I had left the church at 18, free to live my life as I saw fit, wearing red clothing was still taboo for me. I was a sinner. Yahweh forbid the rapture happened, and Jesus came back, and I was wearing red clothing, fingernails, and red lipstick, it was a chance I'd rather not take. So, when my friend asked me to participate, to say I was nervous and judgmental is an understatement. I asked, "Your pastor lets you wear red?" She said, "Where have you been for the last 20 years? That is old timey. The church has changed. We wear red. We see it as a testimony unto God." During those 20 years, I dedicated my life to Christ, earned a masters and doctorate and still believed that wearing red would send you to hell. Hesitant at first, I struggled with accepting the invitation. When I tell you I struggled with the request to wear red, I almost canceled the engagement. Yahweh in His infinite wisdom asked me a question, "Tell me about Jezebel."

After contemplating on the question for some time, I soon realized she was a complete mystery to me. I knew nothing about the woman, except for her name and that she was an evil woman that wore makeup. There are a plethora of biblical scholars and historians that study ancient Israel that wrote tremendous commentary and books about the person of Jezebel and the spirit of Jezebel. I chose the Bible as my main source of reference, particularly the books of 1st Kings to unravel the mystery of Jezebel. The Bible was used to indoctrinate me with fear, then it could also free me from erroneous teachings.

Who is Jezebel? Jezebel was the daughter of Ethbal king of Zidion. According to The Easton's Bible Dictionary, and the Lexham Bible Dictionary[14], Ethbal was a priest of Astarte, the moon goddess. Astarte or Ashtoreth was "frequently associated with the name of Baal, the sun-god, the Phoenicians 'chief male deity."[15] Also, she was the wife of the son of Omri, the wicked and evil Israeli king Ahab who reigned over Israel for twenty-two years. Their marriage was a

---

[14] Roden, C. (2016). Jezebel, Wife of Ahab, Daughter of Ethbaal. In J. D. Barry, D. Bomar, D. R. Brown, R. Klippenstein, D. Mangum, C. Sinclair Wolcott, ... W. Widder (Eds.), *The Lexham Bible Dictionary*. Bellingham, WA: Lexham Press.
[15] Baker's Evangelical Dictionary of Biblical Theology. Edited by Walter A. Elwell

58

political arrangement. When the two married, she became queen of all Israel. Arranged marriages was a common practice among the ancient nations. Peace treaties, the promises of protection, economic trading, conquest of nations all done under the guise of arranged marriages. Marriage was a business arrangement. To marry into foreign nations permitted the erection of temples to worship false gods. Yahweh warned the Israelites not to participate in such marriages with people of foreign nations. He called the nation of Israel to be different, He was to be their God, and they were to be His people, but they rejected His sovereignty, did not trust Him, "Give us a King" they cried, we want to be like other nations. They rejected Yahweh. (1 Sam. 8:6). As Yahweh warned, Jezebel persuaded Ahab to raise altars, to build temples and groves unto Baal.

As queen, she promoted false teachings that honored and worshiped Baal. Her prophets pressured the Israelites to worship Baal instead of Yahweh. These opposing factions separated the nation by those who remained faithful to Yahweh and those who chose to worship the Phoenician god Baal. To strengthen her influence, she killed the prophets of Yahweh

59

and shielded and protected the prophets of Baal and Asherah (1 King 18:1-19). Yahweh used Elijah to judge Jezebel Baal and Asherah and those who followed them.

According to the Biblical text, Elijah, challenged 450 prophets of Baal to meet him at Mount Carmel. Speaking to the nation of Israel, he simply asked "How long will you hesitate between two opinions? If Yahweh be God, follow Him; but if Baal, follow him.[16] The followers of Baal prepared their sacrifice and called upon Baal too send fire to consume it. The Bible says that they spent all day calling on Baal, cutting themselves with knives and lancets, but Baal never answered. They did this until the evening sacrifice. When it was Elijah's turn, he first repaired the altar, made a trench, and poured water in the trench at the altar and on the sacrifice, he did this three times until the altar was soaked. Then he called upon the name of Yahweh. Yahweh sent fire from heaven, consuming the sacrifice. When he was done, Elijah killed the prophets of Baal, all 450 of them. Because of Elijah's action, Jezebel sought to kill him. It really is a fascinating story. A must read.

---

[16] *The Holy Bible: King James Version.* (2009). (Electronic Edition of the 1900 Authorized Version., 1Ki 18:21). Bellingham, WA: Logos Research Systems, Inc.

Jezebel was also responsible for having Naboth stone to death. His vineyard was close to the palace of King Ahab. Ahab wanted the vineyard to grow vegetables. Ahab asked Naboth to sell him the vineyard, Naboth declined his request. Ahab instead of accepting no for an answer went home sulking and crying, refusing to eat. When Jezebel asked him what was wrong, he said Naboth refused to sell his vineyard, "Is this how you act as a King?", exclaimed Jezebel. She executed Naboth and gave the vineyard to her husband. (1 King 21:5-25).

She wore makeup, was controlling, practiced witchcraft, participated in the temple as a prostitute and a prophet. Finally, she died at the hands of Jehu her blood was splattered on the wall, and horses trampled her, and her body was eaten by dogs. (2 Kings 9:31-32). Jezebel was a very wicked woman. She murdered people, was controlling, manipulative, waged war against the God of Israel, tempted the people to turn from God to the Phoenicians' gods Baal and Asherah, participated in temple prostitution, and attempted to kill Elijah. For the life of me, I could not figure out from all I read what red had to do with any of her actions. The Bible is not clear if her favorite color was red, if she wore red makeup, or if the priests and prophets of Baal and Asherah wore red. The Bible simply said she painted her face and that is only when she was facing death.

A little more digging for context led me to some historical research. As far back as 5000 years ago, women wore red lipstick to assert their authority. Both men and women of Egypt of certain social status painted their faces. However, the Greeks saw this as the mark of a prostitute. They were the ones who imposed this on ladies of the evening, regulating the wearing of makeup. If they were found not to have on their trademark red lips, they would be arrested and punished for impersonating a lady.[17]

According to a blog posted in Axiology for the introduction of their new product True Red lipstick, in 16th century England, Queen Elizabeth revived red lipstick's popularity with her signature look of alabaster skin with crimson lips. By the 1700's red lipstick was outlawed in England on the basis that women were using cosmetics as a tool to seduce men into marriage. Similar laws prevailed in the United States, where marriage could be annulled if it was

---

[17] Gabriela Hernandez, Classic Beauty: The History of Makeup, 2nd Edition

found that the woman had been wearing red lipstick during courtship.[18] Seriously! By comparison, the Asian culture saw the adorning of red as passionate love, a color of beauty, power, and strength; it also meant new beginnings and prosperity.

My point is, under the influences of inadequate biblical teaching, erroneous interpretation of scripture, and acts of superstition, instituted a system that put stipulations on a color. Yahweh never intended for people to feel ashamed and to question the power of the blood of Jesus. Rarely do I hear sermons preached about the blood of Jesus or hear songs that honor the blood. Because uninformed denominations do not honor the color and ban it from the church, it is taken as a symbol of violence, mostly affiliated with gangs, and convicted felons. Why can I not wear red to represent the blood of Jesus?

---

[18] Axiology Blog/Royalty, Prostitutes, Witches & Movie Star: The History of the red Lipstick November 20, 2017, https://axiologybeauty.com

## Chapter Six: Application of the Blood

I suspect your question is, how do we apply the blood of Jesus in a practical form to any situation, specifically, those situations that are controlled by Satan. We need practical solutions, not theological concepts. Theology teaches that Jesus shed His blood once for the sins of the world and that is all we need to know about it. The danger of that is it becoming an historical fact rather than a present day and potential reality.

Therefore, we are presented with analyzing and supplying the real-world solution to the most cogent question of how one applies the blood of Jesus in his everyday life. In the natural world, we would have no difficulty understanding how to apply an antibiotic to an infection. We would take the antibiotic and wipe, sprinkle, or pour it upon the infection, and the result would be that all germs or living organisms present in the infection would die. The same thing happens spiritually. Whenever Satan is at work, we apply the only corrective antidote there is, and that is Jesus. There is absolutely no alternative, no substitute. Prayer, praise, and worship, all have their part in our approach to God; but the blood of Jesus is the only effectual antidote to corruption.

Satan always tries to take the blood out of our churches, and in some arenas, he has been most successful. If there is no antidote, no counter to his tactics, then he and his demonic forces are free to continue their destruction in spirit, soul, and body. Having concluded, therefore, that the blood of Jesus is our only remedy, how are we to obtain and use it? In the Old Testament, the priest took hyssop and dipped it into the blood and then sprinkled or painted it upon the lintels and doorpost of the houses of the Israelites. But in the spiritual realm, we take the blood by faith, and we speak it, which is intercessory prayer. Each time we speak it, we are applying it, and we are offering the only plea, which can bring any results in intercession.

Think of it this way. The word blood spoken in faith once, is like a pinhead of blood drops upon the opposition we are facing. When a doctor prescribes an antibiotic to treat an infection, it is usually a regiment to be taken over a period of time. It is more than one dose. So, the more we plead/ speak the blood, the more we are applying it, and the more power we are taking away from our opposers. However, we must not fall into vain robotic repetition, as the Pharisees. Pleading the blood robotically is vain, to do so is ineffective and unwise. To the unbeliever, it appears to be foolish. But for the child of Yahweh who speaks the blood in faith, watch for wonderful results to occur. The whole approach is so simple and obvious that I am often amazed that so many people miss it.

During the Old Testament times, the priest offered physical sacrifice of animals. The flesh was burned with fire, but the blood was sprinkled into basins and was used by being sprinkled. Peter tells us that in the times of the New Testament that we are the priests who offer spiritual sacrifices acceptable to God by Jesus Christ. (1 Peter 2:5). Spiritual sacrifices are the New Testament equivalent of the Old Testament physical sacrifices. As a New Testament believer – Priest, we are to take the living blood of Jesus and sprinkle it with our tongues before the Lord. By repeating the word "Blood" immediately, we begin to bring Satan's work in our lives and the lives of our families, communities, and nations into submission and cancel out his evil intentions.

The blood of Abel spoke revenge, but the blood of Jesus speaks peace, pardon, and reconciliation for all who are bound by Satan. As we speak the word of the blood, we must remember that the blood of Jesus carries all the power, Spirit and life that is in Jesus. As the blood of humanity carries life, so does the blood of Jesus as it carries the life of the Son of Yahweh. Each time we say the word blood in faith we are bringing the creative life force of the universe to bear upon Satan's power to steal, kill, and destroy. Once the bloodline is drawn, he must pass over you! I am not meaning to suggest for a moment that the blood does not always avail for you, and that you, therefore, must continually plead the blood to keep yourself covered. What I am saying is that if you apply the blood continually, when you feel that you are being spiritually attacked or are in special need, you are reminding Yahweh that you are trusting in Him. And, believe me, the blood prevails, and it works every time.

## *Chapter Seven: There is Life in the Blood*

Blood is a strange and mysterious substance. In my

correctional duties, I witnessed incarcerated men and women

intentionally use makeshift knifes to cut their wrists, hands,

legs, and other body parts. Sometimes the blood would seep

out in a slow drip, other times it would rush out as a never-

ending geyser. The sight of blood never bothered me until a

particular mental health inmate, I'll name him Walter, decided

one day that he wanted to do a painting in blood, imitating the

primitive style of Jean -Michel Basquiat. Why? Because he

wanted to return to the psychiatric ward to be with his

girlfriend. When the team and I entered his 8 by 10 medical

cell, the walls, ceiling, and floor were covered with his blood;

we were literally waking in a pool of human blood. The thick aroma of fresh wet blood was sickening to my stomach. I could barely keep from fainting. Never in my life had the smell or the sight of blood made me feel as if I would puke. When I asked him why, he looked at me with a smile, I need to get back to her. As I looked at the blood running down the walls and seeping out the door, my hands clap my mouth, for I had never seen such a horrid sight. Miraculously, he and I both survived. But from that day to this one, the sight and smell of blood still turns my stomach.

On the other hand, it may seem as if the sordid side of man likes to see blood such as those who get excited at the site of blood when cheering on a gory scene in a horror film with blood flowing from dead bodies. Or those who are fascinated by the running blood of slaughtered animals. Whatever the case, blood is a mysterious substance.

The Bible does not tell us of the chemical elements of the red and white blood corpuscles, it simply states the life of the living creature is in its blood. (Leviticus 17:11). Leading scientists and researchers agree. In fact, according to a published article, Facts about Blood, by Johns Hopkins, an international leading medical research institution, blood is the life-maintaining fluid that flows through the body's blood vessels: which consist of arteries, veins, and capillaries. The function of the blood is to carry nourishment, electrolytes, hormones, vitamins, antibodies, heat, and oxygen throughout the body while it is responsible for carrying waste matter and carbon dioxide out of the body.[19]

The most amazing thing about blood is its capacity to carry the life of Yahweh. Many have tried to create life without Yahweh, as portrayed in Mary Shelley's fictional character Frankenstein or the modern-day versions of zombies, but they have failed. Notwithstanding, today scientists are still on a mission. They are conducting real-life experiments with new, modern, high-tech cloning laboratories, in an effort to create life, and they have made some amazing discoveries, such as the utility and benefit of blood banks and the practicality of keeping blood refrigerated for the treatment of medical conditions. Other areas of research include those conducted in the fields of Hematology DNA, and Genetics. What that says to me is humanity can study it, code it, focuses its research on

---

[19] https://www.hopkinsmedicine.org/health/wellness-and-prevention/facts-about-blood Copyright c 2022 The John Hopkins University, the John Hopkins Hospital Health System.

producing substitute blood components, like platelets, but they cannot synthesize blood or the life that the blood carries. Blood truly is a mystery, and that mystery belongs to Yahweh alone.

The contact between Yahweh and humanity is in the blood. There is only one generator of life and that is Yahweh, and He alone is the author of life. In Genesis 2:7 we come into the knowledge that God created humanity. Man is Yahweh's greatest creation upon the earth and was made in His likeness. The Bible teaches that humanity is fearfully and wonderfully made (Psalm 139:14), an even better model than the angels, who represent another creation from Yahweh. Angels are spiritual and not made of flesh, thus no blood because only that which is flesh has blood. With His own hands, Yahweh created humanity. He formed mankind from the substance of which He created the earth. He then breathed into him His very own breath. In other words, Yahweh breathed into this clay, earthen, dirt-formed body, particles of Himself. His very own spiritual life, and the life He created is held in the substance we call blood. Therefore, blood is not life, it carries life. It is not just a statement of faith. Yahweh has given scientists the ability to prove His word. It is widely proven when one expires, the person is still warm and will remain warm for a brief time. However, the essence of life has departed from the blood. We can dress the body up, stage it any way we choose, invite our family and friends to view, but it remains a lifeless corpse, as it has no blood in it. The life of humanity is carried in the blood. Life itself is spiritual, but it must have a physical carrier, and this carrier is the blood.

So how than, do we explain this unique nature of the blood of Jesus Christ. We were long taught in middle school health class that the basic fundamentals of conception is the reproductive process from which babies are born and those teachings have been verified by leading scholars like those at Oxford University (Yan, 2017).[20] If these conceptions are by in-vitro fertilization, or natural coupling the following is known: the female ovum itself has no blood and neither does the male sperm; but it is when they come together in the fallopian tube that conception happens, and a new life begins. The fetus creates its own blood as it receives genes from each parent from which it will create its own cells and blood type! A fetus evolves in the womb all by itself as the mother feeds and

---

[20] Yan, Wei and Clarke, Hugh, The New Chapter for Biology of Reproduction, Biology of Reproduction, Volume 97, Issue 1, 2017, Page 1.

shelters it. Thereafter, this new life is then protected by the mother's placenta from the flow of the mother's blood into the fetus and the wonderful creation of life begins…amazing, is it not! A simple middle school health class lesson about the reproductive system has proven the authenticity of the Word of God. The Bible is explicit and clear that the Holy Spirit is the divine agent responsible for the conception of Jesus in the womb of Mary. It was not a normal conception but a supernatural act of God, planting His Son Jesus, in the womb of Mary. A mystery!

The blood type of the Son of God was and is a special type, and according to the scientists, the following is true. Again, and I emphasis, the mother's ovum has no blood, the blood of the child is determined at conception, and the placenta protects the child from receiving the flow of blood from the mother. Therefore, all the child's blood, in this instance, came from His Father in heaven by a supernatural creative act of Yahweh, which also means that Jesus' blood was without the Adamic stain of sin. Some will argue that Mary supplied the ovum, and the Holy Spirit supplied the spiritual sperm which would mean that Jesus would have been conceived with mixed blood, part Adam part Yahweh. That within itself would have been in violation of Yahweh's plan of salvation for fallen humanity. Others of the metaphysical bloodless cults would argue that Jesus did not exist prior to His conception.

Yahweh in His infinite wisdom records in His word, that He prepared a body for His Son. It was that body that was created in Mary's womb. "Wherefore when He cometh into the world, He saith, sacrifice and offerings thou would not, "But a body hast thou preparest me." (Hebrews 10:5). Jesus, the Son, knew before birth that Yahweh, the Father, would prepare Him a body. He simply came down from heaven and entered the new body created in the womb of Mary. His body had the blood type of God running through His veins, which was not an intermixing with the stained blood of Adam. Jesus, the only begotten of Yahweh the Father, (John 1:14) and His body were formed in the womb of Mary, but the Life that was in Jesus Christ came from Yahweh, the Father, by the Holy Spirit. The life that flowed in the veins of Jesus came from Yahweh. Jesus, in His own words "...I am Life" (John 11:25). Jesus was created perfect and without sin. He was sinless, no sin in His blood. He allowed His sinless blood to be shed for humanity, who had become sinful.

What would the researchers, the scientists, the doctors, the blood banks, and the hospitals give for just one drop of Jesus' blood? Imagine this. All of those who would receive a transfusion would receive the pure blood of Jesus and, consequently, Yahweh's eternal life. Obviously, Yahweh never intended to administer His redemption plan by blood transfusion! But imagine how a greater miracle unfolds, when one trusts in Jesus and accepts Him as His personal Savior. Immediately, a spiritual transfusion takes place as the sin that dwells within us is purged. "For I will cleanse their blood that I have not cleansed: for the Lord dwells in Zion" (Joel 3:21).

# *About the Author*

Dr. Valerie Arthur is Founder and CEO of Christ Centered in the City International Ministries, the non- profit arm of Black Gold International in the USA and Haiti. Dr. Arthur is a charter member and Board Chair of the Smith Family Foundation of New Jersey.

After 27 years of distinguished service with the New Jersey Department of Correction, Dr. Arthur retired as the first African American Administrator in the 100-year history of the Edna Mahan Correctional Facility for Women.

Dr. Arthur believes that God has called her to a unique position to unite and strengthen the body of Christ. She accomplishes this through transformational leadership development, cultivating relationships, and education.

Dr. Arthur received her Doctor of Ministry degree focused on Prison Policy and Transformative Justice from the New Brunswick Theological Seminary.

Dr. Arthur has 3 children and 5 grandchildren.